River
of
Light

River of Light

poems by
Daniel Thomas

SHANTI ARTS PUBLISHING
BRUNSWICK, MAINE

River of Light

Published by Shanti Arts LLC, 193 Hillside Road, Brunswick, Maine 04011; shantiarts.com

Designed by Shanti Arts Designs

Cover image— Frederic Edwin Church, *El Rio De Luz "The River of Light,"* 1877. Oil on canvas. 54.3 x 84.1 inches (138.1 cm x 213.7 cm). National Gallery of Art, Washington, D. C. Public domain.

Interior images—(18–19) Albert Bierstadt, *Yosemite Valley, Glacier Point Trail*, c. 1873. Oil on canvas. 54 x 84.7 inches (137.2 x 215.3 cm). Yale University Art Gallery, New Haven, Connecticut. Public domain. (38–39) Thomas Cole, *View from Mount Holyoke, Northampton, Massachusetts, after a Thunderstorm*, 1836. Oil on canvas. 51.5 x 76 inches (130.8 x 193 cm). Metropolitan Museum of Art, New York City. Public domain. (56–57) John Brett, *Cornwall*, 1897. Oil on card. 9.8 x 17 inches (24.6 x 43.1 cm). Private collection. Public domain.

Bashō quotes are from *Narrow Road to the Interior and Other Writings* by Matsuo Bashō, translated by Sam Hamill. Copyright © 1998 by Sam Hamill. Reprinted by arrangement with The Permissions Company, LLC, on behalf of Shambhala Publications Inc., Boulder, Colorado, shambhala.com.

Quote from Dante's *Divina Commedia* are used with permission of the translator, Michael F. Meister. dantecomedy.com

Quote from *Causae et Curae* by Hildegard of Bingen is used with permission of the author, who produced the translation used herein.

Printed in the United States of America

ISBN: 978-1-962082-85-3 (softcover)

Library of Congress Control Number: 2025946193

This book is dedicated to
my children Gabe, Jamie and George,
and in loving memory of my sister,
Sandra Lee McKay.

Contents

DELTA

ACKNOWLEDGMENTS

The author wishes to thank the editors of the following publications in which these poems first appeared, sometimes in altered form or under different title:

Anacapa Review: "In the Harbor"

Amethyst Review: "Green Pearls"

California Quarterly: "At His Father's Bedside" and "My Daughter is Pregnant"

Front Porch Review: "Birthday Bowl"

Great Lakes Review: "The Narrow Road North"

Midwest Zen: "Practicing" and "What Evening Can't Dispel"

Out of the Ground: Poems Inspired by the Santa Barbara Botanic Garden (Anthology published by Gunpowder Press)*:* "Suns and Shadows" and "Viriditas"

SALT: "At Dawn and at Dusk" and "For a Spell"

San Pedro River Review: "The Fado Singer"

Sheila-Na-Gig: "Pouring Honey"

Still Point Arts Quarterly: "Two Horses"

Thin Places and Sacred Spaces (Anthology published by Amethyst Press): "Intimations"

Timada's Diary: "Of Music and Light"

Vita Poetica: "Snow"

SPECIAL THANKS

I am very grateful for the many teachers, mentors, and fellow poets who have worked with me along the way. I especially want to thank Skip Renker, my poetry soul-brother, for our many years of exchanging poems. And thanks to Thomas R. Smith, for decades of inspiration and support. Many thanks also to Christine Brooks Cote for her generous guidance in the making of this book.

Finally, I am filled with gratitude for my family—my children Gabe, Jamie, and George, their partners and children. I am ever grateful to my siblings—Jo, Sandy, Jim, Mike—and their families. And I was blessed from the beginning thanks to my parents, George and Evelyn Thomas, who modeled for me patience, grace, and kindness.

. . . For I have learned
To look on nature, not as in the hour
Of thoughtless youth; but hearing oftentimes
The still sad music of humanity,
Nor harsh nor grating, though of ample power
To chasten and subdue. And I have felt
A presence that disturbs me with the joy
Of elevated thoughts; a sense sublime
Of something far more deeply interfused,
Whose dwelling is the light of setting suns,
And the round ocean and the living air,
And the blue sky, and in the mind of man:
A motion and a spirit, that impels
All thinking things, all objects of all thought,
And rolls through all things.

—WILLIAM WORDSWORTH, "Lines Composed
a Few Miles above Tintern Abbey"

As a flash of lightning will so blind
the eyes that even the clearest objects
will fade for a moment, just so

I was suddenly enveloped in such a glorious
effulgence of living light that all I could see
was light. And I heard Beatrice say:

"This is how the Love that rules this heaven greets
all who enter here. In this way you are
the candle made ready for its flame."

—DANTE, *Divina Commedia*, "Paradiso: Canto 30,"
translated by Michael F. Meister

GREEN PEARLS

When illness stills you, and worry weights
your limbs—when you rub your eyes to wake up

and the rose light of evening slants
across the dusty table—you take a walk,

but the neighborhood is empty—even the birds
have flown, taking with them the furnishings

of sound that make the world inhabitable.
You remember Midwest autumns—how herds

of maple leaves skittered across the blacktop.
Nestled among tree trunks and leafless shrubs,

they found their place of winter rest.
You, too, hurry down the driveway, brittle

as the dried husk of a seed pod. But within you—
green pearls in a frail shell.

HEADWATERS

A GATHERING OF BLESSINGS AND GRIEF

I TAKE AN EMPTY BOAT, DRIFTED
TO SHORE, AND GO LOOKING FOR YOU

Once, at this very lake, I saw
a woman standing on the bridge
where a stream fed the waters.

She gazed quietly towards
the other shore, but as I walked past,
she turned and smiled at me

and that smile was so genuine
and deep, it felt as though
you were looking through her eyes

and saying I see you. And so,
without looking for you,
I found you, or better, saw you

see me. So now, what more
do I need? If I saw you in a stranger's
eyes, love connecting us

for an instant as our paths crossed,
never to cross again,
what am I still seeking in the lake

of my body? And can I
push the boat through
the reeds and weeds cluttering my heart?

THE FADO SINGER

The word itself contains shadows,
as if the singer stands poised
between the saddened past
and the always fickle future, in a now
lit only by a glaring spotlight
that shines the sequins of her silver
dress and deepens the night sky
hidden in her eyes of black onyx.
Her long arms gesture to the balcony
and her voice trembles through
a languid melody in a minor key,
while three guitars pluck percussive
notes that frame her liquid arcs
like the simple setting of a fine
carnelian stone. Her Portuguese words
grant me liberty to hear only
rhythm and melody and the mouthed and trilled
consonants and vowels that might speak
of lost love, or death beside us
in the dim hall, or the deep sorrow
in these things we live beside. And so
I am transfixed by the origin of drama,
before plot or theme, just
the one life that shines through
her face, stares into darkness, sings
the pure song of our dangling fate.

ABOVE THE MOLTEN CORE

For the one who won't allow herself to eat,
the one who drinks and abandons his children,

the one whose manic fevers secretly delight her,
a spiny knot forms in the folds of the brain.

For the one who lost a son, the one stricken
by a mother or father, the one whose husband

forgets her name, pain becomes a maze
of memories, time a collapsing road.

Each person's grief hides in matter
itself, in molten rock far below.

And in the mountain's dark tunnel, cars
pass through eons of aggregated grief,

held like fists of quartz in stubborn stone.
Stone holds all against forgetting.

I taste it in the teeth, while the mountain
flowers like a tree of sorrows.

TO BE WITHIN THE GLANCE OF BEAUTY

Arles, 2023

Van Gogh propped his easel throughout
the town, painting a yellow
house, a busy café, the Rhône
sparkling under exploding stars.

In focused agitation, he jabbed
and smeared pigments onto
canvas—windows opening
into realms of feeling.

A dog lifts a leg to pee
on the walls of the Roman arena
where gladiators fought and died.
He sniffs the air, alert.

A woman holds the leash, stares
into the elsewhere of her phone,
until Van Gogh's ghost
whispers in her ear.

Dusk is thick with the heavy
weight of lifted stones.
Swallows trace lassoes of light
over darkening rooftops.

TWO HORSES

Most days, we walk together,
passing the field where wildflowers
mingle in the breeze. Some swell
with new buds, others face
the sun in full bloom, or turn
heavy heads downward and wilt
into seed. We veer through
the oak grove by the museum,
and the last stretch before home
takes us by a tiny ranch,
holdover from the rural past,
with a riding pen just big enough
for two horses to circle. Beside it,
a brown horse and a white horse
stand quietly in their pens.
Hand in hand, we watch: the dusty
hooves, the downturned eyes
settled in being—
in sun, grass, breeze, silence.

IN THE STREAM

Beside a mountain brook
a hummingbird
hovers above still
shallows, then dips his body
into water, wings
fluttering the flux, head
bobbing above the ripples—
a wind-up bath
toy splashing along—
until he flits up,
sits on a branch, drips,
then floats above the branch
to dry, stirring wings
in sunshine, his iridescent
feathers a blur against
the still, blue sky.

AT HIS FATHER'S BEDSIDE

While he wondered if he should hold his hand,
grace-notes began to fall from a cloud's

dark brow. And then rain fell in great
swoons of darkness, morning light erased.

Lightning flickered high, while low black
clouds raced like stampeding horses.

Rain streamed down the cliffs of windows
until, like a king weary of raging, the storm

turned away. Sunlight found earth again
and birds sang the world into sodden gladness.

He wondered if he should hold his father's hand,
as a breeze blew droplets from gleaming leaves.

DEATH REFUSES HIM

Near Gaviota, where the 101 passes
through ranch country, hillsides pressed between
the Santa Ynez mountains and the sea, he lounges
on the highway shoulder, head propped on a green
backpack, legs reaching toward the sun-
brushed water. Nothing matters in the sunshine,
the car rush, the salt-breeze, the rosy
autumn light of tilting earth, no better
place to breathe the last breath. Ready
to go, he reviews his wandering travels, itinerant
joys—fourth grade recess on spring
fields, his mother making pancakes for lunch,
the fiery Irish girl he first fell for,
the languor of her lips beneath the oaks,
railroad jobs and the L.A. port, his distant
daughter he hardly knows. Sometimes, after
drinking with friends, he would drive his mother's car
back to her house on a moonlit school night, headlights
off, the car streaking along the dark
nerve of the highway, surf glimmering below
the cliff, and as the speed approached 100,
everything breathed the starry air, everything
blazed in the dark moment, ready to be
released. When headlights criss-cross
four lanes, when three crows settle
on fence posts across the highway, when frigid
ocean air falls on thin clothes
and the bone-weary body refuses to give up,
he starts the long walk south—breathing,
breathing, despite everything, breathing.

MYSTERIES WITHIN

A wand stabs my ribs
and opens my chest
into grainy images.

Hidden caves harbor
a pulsing fist, unlikely
flumes and spillways,

fluttering moths—
limpid ghost wings
trapped in a bone cage.

Flaws appear
in the mechanics of being.
The spark winds down.

Like a sandcastle in sunlight,
the foundation crumbles.
But at the still core,

desire shimmers—
my life a lingering
morning dream.

SUNS AND SHADOWS

Bees bustle between
the dark purple primrose

and the shining orange tree,
from lofty white blossoms

destined to be miniature
suns, to violet flowers,

content to glow in shadow.
They sip the sweetness of each.

MY DAUGHTER IS PREGNANT

My daughter is pregnant with what will be
her second child and, after dinner, stretches
out on the couch, head in her husband's lap,
tired of caring for one child while carrying the other.

My granddaughter and I play on the floor,
while two pups wrestle in the space
around us, stopping from time to time
to lick our faces, nibble our ears.

It's 7:30 on a Saturday night and this
is life for all of them, in the lighted
living room of a small white house
on a quiet street of a big city

in the center of a country of three hundred
million on a blue orb that travels around
the sun in a tiny galaxy among countless others,
and each life coming somehow from something

and going somehow to somewhere,
and each day, each moment in this fertile
abundance, unique and never-to-be-repeated,
the child within her

restless as a summer field at twilight.

POURING HONEY

Like a slow-motion wave,
it gently turns over
on itself, crawls towards
the lip, then crests and drifts
downward, the slow unfolding
of its fall. It quietly drapes itself
over the strawberries and yogurt,
like a blanket drawn across
a sleeping child, and when
I turn the jar to curb
its flow, it makes a long,
delicious curve back
onto itself, skirting
the lip, like a girl in a swing
who relishes the pause
at the very top, before
floating back down.
Can I live like this?
To hold the undeserved
blessings of a thousand blossoms,
pocket the peak of their quick
beauty, their gleaned light,
then open myself with the passing
years, slowly unfolding
from within, to coat
my ragged world and the ones
I love with every last
sweetness.

SNOW

Once in awhile, I see a white-
crested mountain and think of snow.
But distant snow is abstract and aloof.
It doesn't frost your hair, smudge
your glasses, crunch beneath your feet
or slide you down a slick hill.
Sometimes, I think snow is the breath
of the Holy One, lavishing the world
with love—the driveway weighted down
with love, love causing chaos
on sidewalks and streets, walkers slipping
in its thick slush, tires spinning
in its slick slur, schools closed,
errands lost, before plows arrive
to tame footloose love, scrape
its velvet swaddle from the earth,
shove its heaped excess aside,
tear the blizzard's wild fur
from misty eyes, banish the snow-
blind to cold and distant mountains.

BIRTHDAY BOWL

Is there any sound quite like the cacophony
of a bowling alley? . . . the din of balls smashing
pins that crash and tumble on a wood floor?
. . . or the sad sound when a ball slips into
the gutter, then thunks the gulley at the lane's end?
This continuous clamor, punctuated by shouting
and laughter, is so deafening that one tiny
six-week old, hidden behind a blanket
in his stroller, sleeping, perhaps dreaming
beneath the delicate blue veins of his closed
eyelids, one new person named "Eddie,"
sighs himself out of a deep sleep.
He must be shocked to wake to this wall of sound
unmuffled by the gauzy waters of the womb.
His face frowns, lower lip sagging,
before the first cry comes out, but when
it does it's a shriek filled with dismay
that even the new mother and father cannot
dissuade. They take turns passing him back
and forth as they continue their game—this special
afternoon a story to be told to him
some day—the father's birthday, the older children,
a family with a new member, the beer and cheese
curds, the lonely fellow, whose only comfort
in this crazy place is the warm, full breast
of his mother, but she, wearing her two-tone
bowling shoes and gliding towards the line,
just needs a good roll to pick up a spare.

AFTER THE RAIN

We wait and wait through days of drought.
Dust smothers every surface—
a coat of grime on windowsills
and chairs, a sandpaper grit
that grinds and sharpens every edge.
I long for liquid days, the soaking
shower that rinses away the thin
film that separates all things.

Come, rain, and darken the relentless
sun, wash away the light, sodden
every parched skin, so when you cease,
earth becomes a gleaming shelter, where even
the darkest corner glimmers and glows,
the world finally shining from within.

FRUITS OF THE EARTH

1

The people wandering lost in the desert
were blessed with seven species, blossomings
of their love for the One they worshiped
who left them to sift their souls through
countless grains of sand. Wheat and barley
were the grains that waved in the fields,
harvested at Passover and Shavuot.
Grapes formed the fermented gift of wine.
Figs were pressed into cakes. Pomegranates
flavored their dishes. Dates were made into honey,
which sweetened the day. Olives and olive oil
were the core of cooking, and light itself. These
were the fruits of love for a people who stubbornly
clung to the life of the soul in an arid land.

2

Far from the land of exile where a people
wandered in the desert, far from city highways
and cracked sidewalks, in a lush land of green
hills, where stubborn crusts of snow disappear
in spring and swell rivers, the humble trees
line the fields, red or yellow or green
globes within easy reach, Empire and Braeburn,
Cortland and Gala, Macoun and Ambrosia,
too many types to name, and each with a history
and purpose—pie or cider, biting or canning—:
they are the commoners of the land, the people's
most plebian friends, at home in the child's lunchbox
or the chef's salad, they surrender their skin to our teeth,
their tart or sweet flesh to expectant tongues,
they nestle in the pockets of ordinary days,
self-packaged and waiting to be useful.

3

There's something personal, no, intimate, about you—
your soft, sweet flesh, your voluptuous fullness,
your blushing skin, alive with downy hair,
your suppleness that melts into pies or cobblers
or preserves; you are the star of the county fair,
the luxurious dessert in the 5-star Italian restaurant,
the sensual bounty of tiny trees, blossom of pink
and white flowers, metaphor for delicateness
itself; were you not invented by a God
who must love the sweet juiciness of fruit,
we would have to wish you into being ourselves,
hiding you from the jealous eyes of the One
who guided the lost tribe into the Promised Land
and made every perfect tenderness, but somehow
missed this most human fruit of the spirit.

CONFLUENCE AND FLOW

AT DAWN AND AT DUSK

Day came with a delicate
stream of light—brickwork
brushed with the orange refraction
of the sun's relentless awareness—
a sunrise quiet as first
blush on a farmland valley.
But soon, morning began
to spin like a washer wringing
night from day, and soon
the swirl of blood and time
and forgetfulness. Now,
I walk along the shoreline
between beach and street,
and listen to waves wash,
seagulls screech. Beside
their van, men speak
quietly of the day's surf.
A woman sits, dog
in lap, staring out
at the sea. Three pelicans
and a flock of seagulls stand
at the water's edge, watching
each wave roll in. As the sun
slowly dissolves, leaving
behind an ochre aura,
dog, woman, pelicans,
seagulls float between day
and night, sand and sea,
silence and speech, self
and other—this moment
between, soaked in stillness,
caught in muted shine,
held in the mind's gauzy
net, yet slipping
through its open mesh.

HOME REPAIR

It was only after I
painted the eaves, polished
the storm windows, scrubbed

the deck, cleared the gutters,
and caulked the roof, only after
the help desk at Home Depot

knew me by name, and my love
said "sit down and rest,"
only after I took five pills

from the Monday door
of the SMTWThFS pillbox,
only then did I realize

that neither I nor my house,
neither timber nor flesh,
neither fibrous planks and beams,

cellulose of years—stronger
in death than living human
flesh—nor my own thin being

would stand forever, and so
bowing my head to that vandal
time, I pulled up a chair and sat.

NAKED IN THE GARDEN

As forgotten possessions
emerge from the back closet
and the kitchen's high cupboard,
moving brings both
chaos and clarity.

Burdened by the shell
he cannot carry, the snail
goes naked in the garden.

So I try to quiet
the incessant chatter
in my head,
the ego's lurching
never-weary voice.

I sweep the clutter out
of my mind and the ego
asks: what's left of *you?*
can the Holy One find you
in your empty room?

PRACTICING

Past the room where bodies bob to pounding
music   trapped in spinning contraptions

and the one where steely people
grunt confronting dark weights

I roll out my mat in a bare room
and follow the guiding voice until

the mind gives in to wholly
listening   and curbed

by a meditation on muscle and bone
merges with flesh.

Walking home   limber and loose
my shadow rushes ahead.

WHAT EVENING CAN'T DISPEL

Though day pursues
its varied duties, evening
lies down without care.

The flock of blackbirds
settles on the meadow. Rain
brushes the veiled lake.

The shadow at your feet
melts into the moment.
When the cricket sings,

trees quiet their leaves.
Moonlight muffles
clocks and bells.

Only the screech owl insists
on calling out its name
through each dark hour.

FOR A SPELL

Time has turned her bones brittle,
shriveled her muscles and bent her back
to bowed submission. Her legs stiffly

shuffle. Her white hair is stuffed
beneath a knitted cap. As slow
falling snow fills rutted

roads and woods, blurring shapes,
the landmarks of her life whiten, the house
of memory lightens and floats away.

Who remembers her landing naked
in her mother's arms? Or loving the boy
across the street? She lived in rushing

moments, a steady stream seldom
paused. Old woman, once
a child, what keeps you alive keeps me—

scent of salt air by the sea,
hooting owl in dark trees,
butter melting into toasted bread—

fleeting beauty in a transient realm.
We pause before this now needing
nothing, find we're out of time.

IN MIDWEST SUMMER

Under the parsimonious skies
of California, eyes lift and hopes
rise when the sky darkens,

and sometimes drizzle seems
to fall but disappears
in the thirsty air before it lands.

Other days clouds move on
like drifters in a boxcar, watching
the worn-out world go by.

Far away in Midwest summer,
thunderstorms roll in, hang
around Main Street, gunning

their engines, then move on to other
towns. Rain falls, generous
as good cheer, lakes lounge about,

serene in their belonging.
Abundance rests between their shores,
blue as the washed summer sky.

THE NARROW ROAD NORTH

From the earliest times there have always been some
who perished along the road.
            —Matsuo Bashō (translated by Sam Hamill)

1

After two and a half hours of Minnesota flatlands,
the car slowly climbs the long western ridge
of glacial strata, until the great lake
bursts into view—bridges and ore docks
laid like toys across the broad cloth
where the St. Louis River widens to the bay
among the dingy houses of west Duluth.

I rent a cabin at water's edge, my companions
moss-covered boulders, ancient white pines,
books, coffee, bananas and bug spray.
Leaf shadows shimmer the table.

> Open a little space
> when you are nowhere
> and you can be now here.

2

I set my tools of awareness on the kitchen
table—this simple sound box
of paper and pen, strings stretched
across the body of the world.

> The apple tree's green globes sway.
> A crow carries the night sky.
> Even the sun has somewhere it has to go.

> But the yellow tulip cups
> three dew-drops—balanced
> on a thin green stem for a slender time.

3

In the lapping blue well, I lose
my self, like ink seeping into
paper's clean indifference—
and emptied of self, my being fills
with world, an osmosis of perception.

> Today is the ticking kitchen clock,
> lake swells, breathing in and out.
> The robin sings of nothing but today.

4

Language transforms landscape.
When *bay* becomes *harbor*, breakwaters appear,
a lighthouse rises at the peninsula's point,
boat slips slide along shore. Train tracks stretch
over water, carrying ore from Iron Range mines
to this westernmost tip of the Great Lakes.

Old-timers drive their trucks to Agate Bay
to watch the ore ships come and go.
And the vast vista of water slaps
and complains at shore, heaves and sinks beyond,
resigned to its limits — no place to go.

> We are boats in the harbor, each
> distinct, but each leaving a wake
> that widens, quells, disappears.

5

Meaning takes its flavor from layers
of burnish and shine, the sheen of hands
holding each word like a pump handle
or ploughshare's grip, worn with fingerprints,
fragrant with work, the sunlit presence
of long-gone lives.

> Words like yellowed oars,
> blades wet and shining, lapped by
> the many meanings of lake.

6

The sound of surf filters through pine trees
to the needle-covered car. I pack it
in darkness for the drive south to the Twin Cities.
As I follow the gravel road back to the highway,
tires crunch, headlights search. I drive an hour
beneath the half moon and brightening
east, then pull off at a rest stop.

> This misty morning, maple leaves
> circle the tree trunk—bright
> syllables naming the dawn sky.

OPEN YOURSELF TO RECEIVE

To be fertile ground, loosened
and unlatched, cleared of stubborn
rocks, mulish expectations.

To be without the needy
thinness of sand, the clay
of greed in all its dense desire.

To lie open to each penetration
of the sun, arrows of birdsong—at rest
beyond the spectral grasping of the mind.

To quell the nervous disposition,
the longing for approbation. To seek
the god of fullness by praising the god

of emptiness. Perhaps then, like moonlight's
softest glimmering on a shard of polished
onyx, a seed falls and finds a place

in the waiting field; it cracks years
of sedimentary layers, burrows and sprouts,
offers fruit to each passing traveler.

IF JUST BRIEFLY

New Year's first snow—ah—
just barely enough to tilt
the daffodil
            —Matsuo Bashō (translated by Sam Hamill)

The bike shadow and flat
figure hunched above it
glide along the smooth
blacktop. Shadow spokes
spin. Shadow shapes
follow the path's black
branches and patches of light.

A flickering movie unspools
through morning woods as the self
slips into the moment
and suffering fades.

In Stevens' supreme fiction,
imagination conjures
the shadow play
that attenuates the noisy self,
if just briefly, so song
and gratitude can be
discovered.
            Be silent.

Look and listen. Let
the senses fill. The daffodil
with morning snow.

THE BOOK OF SNOW

Beside the frozen lake,
sunlight draws shadows
of naked trees across snow,
streams and tributaries
of leafless branches become
the sure lines of a Japanese drawing—
black ink arcing
across a clean white sheet.

Now, plump snowflakes
land on the wooden fence,
top the long rails,
rise from fenceposts, like tall,
white hats, and soon
a bright fence doubles the brown.

In the children's snow angels,
a spirit world, written
in snow, slowly fills and fades.

And as the sun begins
its afternoon decline
the lines that filled the lake's
boundless pages dim,
disappear like
misty winter breath.

So things grow,
things disappear;
in the soft, white snow,
what's lost is near,
what's found will soon go.

HAKONE, JAPAN

On the way to Lake Ashi,
near Hakone, the bus climbs
a winding mountain road, passes
through wind-swept curtains of fog,
while dark clouds swirl above.

Down by the lake in the hot spring,
sprinkles of rain cool my shoulders
and head. The hillside above is dotted
with swaying pine trees
and one cherry blossom tree.

When the clouds break for a moment,
pink blossoms shine in sunlight
and a breeze wafts a few petals
down to the steaming water.

Cherry blossom tree
Trembling in the hot spring
Petals cling to my knee

NARA, JAPAN

I walk in afternoon drizzle
to Todaiji Temple.
Puddles dot the gravel path,
moss greens stone lanterns,
wet leaves and pine needles
glisten in the woods—:
a light within the wet world glows.

In a wooden structure—roof held aloft
by broad columns of joined cypress—
the huge bronze Buddha glimmers.
Next to Buddha is Guanyin—a bodhisattva
who embodies compassion—the one
who hears the cries of the world.
One hand is open on her lap,
the other raised as if in greeting
and a gold aura surrounds her shoulders,
beams of light blazing from it.

Everyone I know and love
is asleep on the far side
of the shadowed earth,
and all the space between
filled with the cries of the world.

RYOANJI TEMPLE

for Sandy

The elegant emptiness of the rock garden's
raked sand and arranged boulders
is spread before a wash of green.
The grounds around the temple glow

with the gardener's handiwork—praise
made by nurturing and pruning
ever-changing forms and colors,
as leaves sprout, needles fall,

light blooms or dims. Walking
the garden, we are hushed by the sacred,
as if walking through a stone
cathedral, but these living stones

breathe as no cathedral does.
In the grove behind the temple, hidden
among whispering leaves, an old
fountain plays its water flute.

A faded wooden sign says:
"I only know I have enough."

DELTA

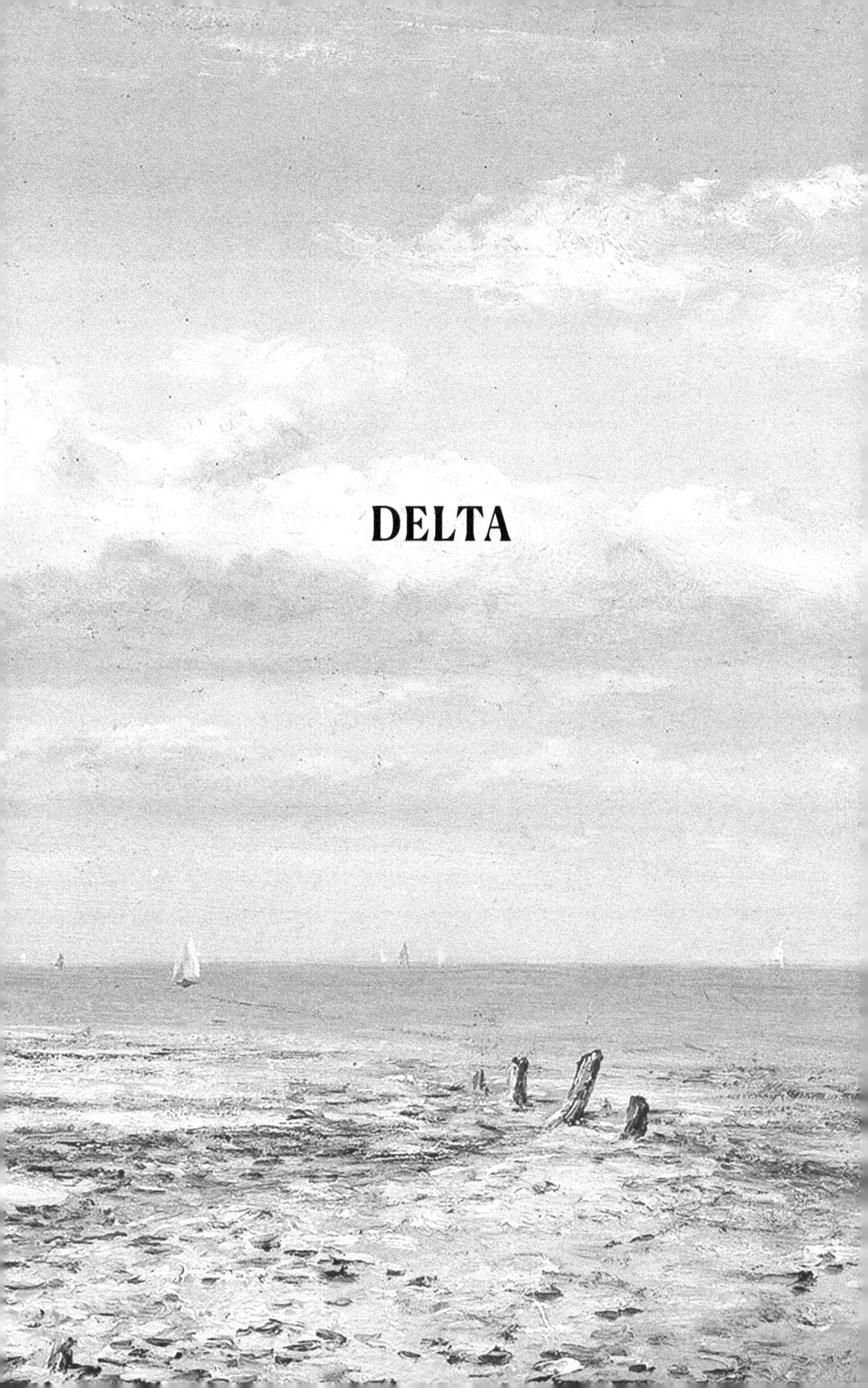

FINDING TIME

So often, when I was young,
I was impatient, in a hurry,
always short on time.

But as I age, water-
striders skim the surface
of the dark memory pond.

So many years I've watched
the sun rise and set,
leaves unfurl, fade and fall.

Now, I sit beneath
a willow, breezes stirring
languid leaves.

As sunshine melts away,
moths gnawing the empty
garments of the waning day,

I lay my head back, gaze up
at the faithful sky, that simply
carries its given light.

OF TIME AND A 1982 MERCEDES

An older man joyfully steers
his 1982 Mercedes around
a corner, top down, wind
fluttering his hair and quivering
the silver cottonwood leaves.

What will he do now
in 1982, and how will he ever
return from the spell of a long-ago
day, slowly driving back
through monsoons of time?

Buddhists say time is an illusion,
and past and future only
barriers to seeing the now,
though other people say
time is a raging river that even

the Army Corps of Engineers can't
tame—its relentlessness won't
be channeled and late in life
it floods its banks and carries us
to great vistas from roofs and treetops.

So what about this man who looks
as if he lives in an interval
of time past? Has he escaped
the rushing current? Must he
face the dogmas of time?

Maybe he sleeps in great
swaths of darkness, blank
as anesthesia's nothingness,
and rises, like Lazarus, morning
after morning, into the perfect day.

VIRIDITAS

Most honored Greening Force that roots in the Sun . . .
You are encircled in divine mysteries.
> —Hildegard of Bingen, *Causae et Curae*

Minnesota-born, I'm like a humdrum
spruce or elm. But in the California
garden store, I find rows of orange
and green seedlings, smooth and prickly mysteries,

humble plants in dusty soil, suffused
with eccentricity, as if the Creator—bored
with shrubs and trees—made stranger things, carved
the thumbs of jade petals, octopus arms of aloes.

For Hildegard of Bingen, the light that inspires
plants quickens the soul, and the soul, she says,
is for the body as the sap is for the tree.

Whether leaves or bristles, flowers or thorns
sprout from us, the one light makes
green things green, animates the seed within.

HOUSE PLANTS

They have modest needs—consistent baths,
a suitable window view, a terra-
cotta house that's comfortably small.

Despite their self-possessed stillness, they depend
on us, and if the vagaries of our lives
cause neglect, they simply wither and die.

They yield to our seclusion from
the natural world, but as I gather them
like a verdant congregation, monks

around the altar of the kitchen sink,
they bow in stoic silence—to the window's
glow, the damp blessings that quicken

their hidden roots—their only ambition
to clutch tightly the earth,
while reaching always for the light.

PULLING WEEDS

Growing from a crack in the garden
wall, a weed lifts
a jagged leaf to the sun.

Though I admire the ingenuity
of wind and seed,
I pull it out, revealing

the slender tendrils of its roots,
and remember how once, as a child,
I touched an elephant's leathery

trunk and looked up into
his eyes, surprised to see
a flourish of lashes, generous

as a beauty queen's, delicate
against his ancient skin.
I learned then of the world's

wild adornments, as now,
so much older, how a plucked
weed can open the garden gate.

OF MUSIC AND LIGHT

"Music is very delicate and it takes, therefore,
  the soul at its softest fluttering to catch these violet
  rays of emotion" wrote Debussy.
                                    But the sound
of Mingus is a house on fire—and mother, father,
sister, brother dancing with orange flames.
They climb to the black roof and rise with smoke
up to a paradise giddy with the counterpoint
of chaos and order.
                          Even those that cannot see
colors in keys are moved by chords that shine
like ragged mountains above the plains: the Tristan
chord from Wagner, Stravinsky's polytonal chords
of Petrushka and Rite of Spring.
                                    I first heard them
as a high school kid, listening with headphones
late at night in my parents' living room—
the delicate drop of needle to spinning track,
hum and buzz settling in the groove,
then crackle and pop accompanying first notes—
a head-bowed genuflection—scotch
and ashtray, Coltrane and Wagner, headphones
draped, pilot on a quiet transatlantic
flight, water glimpsed in amber moonlight.

Listen to the waning sound of a single note
that rings in its unique vibrations. It sets
the invisible air to move, transforms with every
texture it meets, then grazes the gentle membranes
of our inner ears, so we too shake
like the universe, ringing in the one moment
of the one day—its light that slowly fades away.

INTIMATIONS

Twice now I've felt it. The first time
I was driving in a snowstorm. Snow
swirled in the headlights. Snow covered

the trees that stretched above, their white
boughs forming an arch that turned
the road into a softly flurried tunnel.

The second time I was on a small-
town street called Puesta del Sol,
with the sun pouring through palm

and eucalyptus leaves, the whole road
lit with the same gauzy light
as that snowy night, and both times

I felt myself begin to glide, like
a frictionless slide on a long
river of ice, traversing a luminous

channel, a pipeline of light,
where bright, calm, endless time
opened wide on the other side.

IN THE HARBOR

Masts tinted by the setting sun
boats rock beside docks
quiet as a herd
settling down for the night.

Lulled asleep by lapping waves
the tide's soft creep
the boats are horses
tethered to moonlight

dreaming of grassy fields
clear ponds
wind-filled manes
soft earth beneath cloven hooves.

They are dream creatures
lost in dreams of their own
inside the dark harbor—
the whole world floating.

LOST AND FOUND

Lost in the streets of a strange city,
I search for my hotel, its name
and location forgotten, my memory
a locked boathouse without a key.
The woman who stops and offers to help
is my mother, as I've seen her in photos,
in the full bloom of her early twenties,
still in Chicago, in school at DePaul.
She doesn't know my hotel or me,
but walks me to her father's shop
to see if he can help.

As a child I thought heaven was a place
where I would meet famous people—
Magellan or Mickey Mantle.
But in my dream a confounding love waits
at every cloud-wrapped corner. Gliding
beside her, I see her smile as she walks
along, a girlish spring in her step
I've never seen before.

HERE BEFORE ME

Standing on a cliff before the ocean, with—
sun-dazzled face—
briny-breezed nose and hair—
cloud- and sky-mingled water—
pelicans swooping through glitter and sheen—
rising swells, turning wave-tops—
lathered shore—
sky-filled pools—

I stop to think
how words can grasp a portion of this simple scene
brush and paint can trace another part
the most exacting camera perhaps a small piece

but better to surrender
to absolute absorption
and step through this one
of many radiant doors

THE BLUE DOOR

1

The blue door beckons. It drifts in the harbor,
behind the breakwater, among the pleasure boats.
It shines with a kind of warm darkness.

The blue door leads into a small,
floating cabin, hardly big enough
for one person to sit in or lay down.

It has two small windows facing the sea
and when you look out the windows
you see the heaves and swells of eternity.

The blue door is a kind of gate, but it
denies no one entry. It is the only
door into the afterlife and everyone must

seep through the dark shades of its wood.
The blue door is what we will yearn for
when the last hour comes.

On the beach, a bulldozer grooms berms
against the winter storms. Surfers in wetsuits
bob among the swells, watching for waves.

Further out, glints of scalloped edges
surge and sink. But where the land interrupts it,
the water frays into froth and threads. The land

can barely contain the sea's thrashing, its desire
to overrun the earth, to spread its kingdom
of salt and fishes. The blue door beckons.

2

When the phone call came, very early,
that you died in Croatia, the expected became
the unexpected, your inevitable collapse

a shock. For you had such strength of will,
a life force that powered your withered
body across oceans, over hillsides,

through busy cities, your relentless walking
forging on, even as your body began
to bend and stoop and yield to gravity's power.

I think of that picture of you, standing knee-
deep in Lake Harriet. You were a teenager
with all the loveliness we do not know

we own at that age—the soft skin
of hands and arms, gentle sculpting of new
knees. And you had something more—

a classic beauty of face and form,
a confidence in stance and gesture.
But you saw your body differently.

At the end you were already a kind of pure
spirit—mind and will carrying a frail,
62-pound body—and it seemed as though

you could sustain that act of levitation
forever. And then one day you couldn't—
your body collapsed, and lying alone

on the floor of a bathroom, you and your spirit left us,
sliding away into the shadowy realm of memory—
death like a swarm of grasshoppers decimating
a field, or an ocean wave swamping a canoe,
or just the intermittent cries of cicadas
ushering in a summer day in a faraway land.

LIGHT

*But when anything is exposed to light, it becomes
visible, for anything that becomes visible is light.*
—Eph. 5:13–14 (ESV)

If anything that becomes visible is light,
then we and all the world are light—
we are emanations, wave, radiance.
And what if no light is ever lost
but travels through space forever, an eternal
illumination, the brightness of our frail
substance shining always
somewhere, wherever a confluence
of radiance takes place. And call
this gathering of radiance the afterlife—
or, as some prefer, heaven—for there
we will see clearly face to face,
the luster of the visible shining upon
the visible, unobstructed by the murkiness
of the material. Some say we will see
the face of the Creator, but the face
of the Creator is the sum radiance
of everything that shines, and every
thing shines, every thing at the core
of its being is light, the one One
is light. So even if there is no
afterlife like what we may have been
led to expect, let us praise
the lowly beetle, the humble weed,
the abandoned car, the dirty snow
melting in the parking lot, the brown
leaves waving in winter wind, the rainbow
trace of oil on the summer highway,
the lost glove buried in mud,
the bones of the rabbit in the roadside ditch,
the cracked toilet leaning on a fence,

each and every thing that reaches
your eyes and mine, the eyes of us all,
all eyes seeing light, all eyes made
of light, all light, all of this—
the shining face of the Creator.

WHAT DANTE DRANK WITH HIS EYES

A man that looks on glass,
On it may stay his eye;
Or if he pleaseth, through it pass,
And then the heav'n espy.
—George Herbert, "The Elixir"

In this glory of electromagnetic radiation,
light inhabits the water trickling down
Rattlesnake Canyon, living in each runnel,
ripple, winding thread that skirts the naked
rocks, washes the slippery stones, those
bathing beauties imbued with light's liquid
flow. If the Divine is the source of all light—
the fog and salt shoreline dawn, the blaze
of noonday desert sun, the moon-cast
shadowland of prairie fields, the searching
headlights of midnight rural roads—
then painting is the art form closest to God,
for Monet said, "the real subject of every
painting is light." The palette and brushes of heaven's
light paint the visible, but we use them
to paint the invisible, so it appears out
of nothing and stands before us soaked in the mystery
of dream, as Van Gogh's canvas empties
the mind's caverns into a countryside filled
with crows struggling through a liquid sky.

And Rothko's abstracted horizons, El Greco's
stretched holy ghosts, harness the Light
that is the life of all creatures, and create
a field of color, shape and texture that is
a thing resting in itself, and, in this,
is like the sudden and singular vista from a trail
in the Santa Ynez mountains, where the dark
oaks texturing the hills slant toward
the misty ocean shining in the mountain gap.

Standing before the enigmatic pleasure
of a painting, the mind might consider materials
and influence and history, but faced with a new vista,
new entity, new being, the heart
considers only feeling. And as Andrea del Sarto,
the faultless painter, says in Browning's poem,
"Speak as they please, what does the mountain care?"

Vermeer created only thirty-four paintings,
mostly women engaged in household work
in two small rooms of his home and bathed
in the light of ordinary life, Divine light
in domesticity, as Divine love serves
to model what human love might be, and human
love prepares us for transcendent encounters.
Only the living are allowed to see these things.
The dead become them.
                          Led by Beatrice,
Dante enters the "heaven that is pure light"
in Canto 30 of *Paradiso*. She leads
him to the *"lume in forma di rivera"*
and, as illustrated in Blake's watercolor,
Dante crouches in order to drink with his eyes.
Come to me, One Beyond Name,
and fill me with the light far beyond
meaning—photons and waves that charge the thoughtless
now, so it can hold all beauty and pain
in suspension, like a frame around a river of light.

ABOUT THE AUTHOR

DANIEL THOMAS was born in Minneapolis, Minnesota. As an undergraduate at the University of Minnesota, he studied music, English literature, and German literature. He went on to graduate studies in film history, theory and criticism at the University of Wisconsin, Madison. He has an MFA in poetry from Seattle Pacific University.

River of Light is his third collection of poetry. His second poetry book, *Leaving the Base Camp at Dawn*, was published in 2022. His first collection, *Deep Pockets*, won a 2018 Catholic Press Award. He has published poems in many journals, including *Poetry Ireland Review*, *Southern Poetry Review*, *Nimrod*, *Atlanta Review*, and others.

His graduate degree in film led him to Twin Cities Public Television, where he was the video editor of an Emmy Award-winning national PBS series and producer of local documentaries. He went on to become chief operating officer of the PBS station. His long career in nonprofit management includes work as an executive director and a chief development officer.

In addition to writing poetry, he plays the guitar and writes music. For six years he served as vice-chair of the American Composers Forum. His album, *Fur and Feathers*, is available on most streaming services. Dan is the father of three grown children. He moved to Santa Barbara, California, in 2015.

Find poetry, music, and photography at danielthomaspoetry.com.

SHANTI ARTS

NATURE ▪ ART ▪ SPIRIT

Please visit us online
to browse our entire book catalog,
including poetry collections and fiction,
books on travel, nature, healing, art,
photography, and more.

Also take a look at our highly regarded art
and literary journal, *Still Point Arts Quarterly*,
which may be downloaded for free.

www.shantiarts.com

www.ingramcontent.com/pod-product-compliance
Lightning Source LLC
Chambersburg PA
CBHW041720090426
42739CB00019B/3492